March 2012

FEDERAL CONTRACTING

Effort to Consolidate Governmentwide Acquisition Data Systems Should Be Reassessed

FEDERAL CONTRACTING

Effort to Consolidate Governmentwide Acquisition Data Systems Should Be Reassessed

Highlights of GAO-12-429, a report to congressional committees

Why GAO Did This Study

The U.S. Government spends more than $500 billion each year on contracts. To ensure contracts are managed effectively, the government has established policies and procedures for advertising, awarding, administering, and reporting on them. Historically, data systems used to implement these steps have been fragmented and duplicative, with multiple systems across different agencies providing similar services. The Integrated Acquisition Environment (IAE) was initiated in 2001 to bring together different data systems into a unified system. It is intended to reduce duplication and information technology costs, and create a more streamlined and integrated federal acquisition process.

GAO was asked to assess (1) the acquisition strategy being used to develop IAE; (2) progress that has been made in consolidating IAE systems; and (3) any challenges that may affect the completion of IAE. GAO analyzed program costs, schedules, contracts, acquisition documents, and briefings, and interviewed IAE program officials and contractors.

What GAO Recommends

GAO recommends that GSA reassess the IAE business case to determine whether the current acquisition strategy is the most cost effective alternative and if so, reevaluate the current hosting strategy and align contract payments with the program schedule. GSA agreed with GAO's recommendations and indicated that it will take appropriate action.

View GAO-12-429. For more information, contact William T. Woods at (202) 512-4841 or WoodsW@gao.gov.

What GAO Found

The development of IAE has occurred in two stages using different acquisition strategies. In 2001, GSA began establishing a portfolio of standardized government-wide data systems through an acquisition strategy known as "adopt, adapt, acquire." GSA adopted or adapted existing agency-specific systems for government-wide use, or if no viable system met an identified need, GSA acquired a new system. These efforts resulted in a portfolio of nine data systems. In 2008, GSA began consolidating its portfolio of systems into one integrated system called the System for Award Management (SAM). In developing the system, GSA hoped to eliminate redundancy, reduce costs, and improve efficiency. Unlike the existing systems that were each designed, developed, and operated by a single contractor, IAE relies on multiple vendors to perform these same tasks for SAM. The intent of this approach is to enhance competition and innovation and for the government to own the software associated with the system. SAM will be developed in phases. In each phase, capabilities from selected IAE systems will be added to SAM and those legacy systems will be shut down.

GSA has made progress in developing SAM and phase 1, consisting of three systems, is scheduled to be completed in May 2012. GSA also has established a computing center to host SAM and a help desk to support users. Since 2009, however, IAE costs have increased by $85 million, from about $96 to $181 million. Most of the cost growth is due to GSA omitting hardware and other key components in acquiring a hosting infrastructure for SAM. External factors, including recent statutory requirements and policy changes, also have contributed to higher costs by increasing the use of the IAE systems beyond what was anticipated. Higher costs led to the need to supplement existing funding, but the program did not receive all of the additional funding it requested. In response to rising costs and limited funding, GSA officials have delayed SAM's development schedule by almost 2 years, and taken other actions to reduce or defer costs where possible.

Higher costs and constrained resources pose a risk to IAE going forward. GSA will need to continue operating the legacy IAE systems and contend with higher SAM development costs for several more years. While GSA has taken some steps to reduce costs, it has not reevaluated the business case for SAM or determined whether it is the most cost effective alternative. Such a reevaluation is particularly important in light of the increased infrastructure costs, which are now a major impediment to completing SAM. In addition, although the SAM development phases have been pushed out several years, GSA has not modified its primary development contract to align the payment schedule with the delays. The program has continued to pay the same fixed price amount to the contractor for SAM development, operation, and maintenance even though there was little to operate and maintain for nearly 2 years. Aligning contract payments with schedule milestones will ensure that the government is not paying for work that has not yet been accomplished.

Contents

Abbreviations

ACE	Acquisition Committee for E-Gov
CCR	Central Contractor Registration
CFDA	Catalog of Federal Domestic Assistance
CPARS	Contractor Performance Assessment Reporting System
DOD	Department of Defense
DUNS	Data Universal Numbering System
EDS	Electronic Data Systems
EPLS	Excluded Parties List System
eSRS	Electronic Subcontract Reporting System
FAPIIS	Federal Awardee Performance and Integrity Information System
FAR	Federal Acquisition Regulation
FedReg	Federal Agency Registration
FPDS-NG	Federal Procurement Data System – Next Generation
FSD	Federal Service Desk
FSRS	Federal Funding Accountability and Transparency Act Subaward Reporting System
GCE	Global Computer Enterprises
GSA	General Services Administration
HP	Hewlett-Packard
IAE	Integrated Acquisition Environment
IBM	International Business Machines
MOU	memorandum of understanding
OMB	Office of Management and Budget
ORCA	Online Representations and Certifications Application
PPIRS	Past Performance Information Retrieval System
WDOL	Wage Determinations OnLine

United States Government Accountability Office
Washington, DC 20548

March 15, 2012

The Honorable Claire McCaskill
Chairman
Subcommittee on Contracting Oversight
Committee on Homeland Security and Governmental Affairs
United States Senate

The Honorable Darrell E. Issa
Chairman
The Honorable Elijah E. Cummings
Ranking Member
Committee on Oversight and Government Reform
House of Representatives

The U.S. government spends more than $500 billion each year on contracts. To ensure they are managed effectively, the government has established policies and processes for advertising, awarding, administering, and reporting on contracts. These processes use a number of data systems to support each of these steps, from collecting key information from contractors, to evaluating contractor performance, to tracking contract activity. In the past, these systems were fragmented and duplicative, with multiple systems across different agencies providing similar services. In 2001, the Office of Management and Budget (OMB) established an initiative called the Integrated Acquisition Environment (IAE) to unify and integrate different acquisition data systems. IAE is intended to enable agencies to share data and make more informed decisions, make it easier for contractors to do business with the government, and result in cost savings to the taxpayer.

Efforts to develop IAE have been under way since 2001, and you asked that we assess how its implementation is proceeding. In response, we examined (1) the acquisition strategy being used to develop IAE; (2) progress that has been made in consolidating the IAE systems; and (3) challenges that may be affecting the completion of a fully integrated IAE. In order to address these objectives, we obtained and analyzed program documents including cost estimates, schedules, contracts, and internal analyses, and conducted our own analyses of them. We also interviewed officials from the General Services Administration (GSA), the executive agency for IAE, OMB, and the Acquisition Committee for E-Gov (ACE), which is part of the Chief Acquisition Officer's Council and has oversight responsibilities for IAE.[1] We discussed IAE's acquisition strategies over time, the program's current status, including its cost, schedule, and performance parameters, and technical and management challenges that face the program. Finally, we interviewed current IAE contractors to discuss their work on IAE systems and industry practices.

We conducted this performance audit from September 2011 to March 2012 in accordance with generally accepted government auditing standards. Those standards require that we plan and perform the audit to obtain sufficient, appropriate evidence to provide a reasonable basis for our findings and conclusions based on our audit objectives. We believe that the evidence obtained provides a reasonable basis for our findings and conclusions based on our audit objectives.

Background

The federal acquisition process involves a number of steps that are common to all government agencies such as solicitation, evaluation, and contract award. Agencies are increasingly leveraging electronic data systems to streamline acquisitions and reduce costs. According to GSA officials, as these systems gained greater use within the government, some agencies developed their own unique data systems to support acquisition activities. These systems served specific roles in the acquisition process, such as contractor registration or performance tracking. There was little coordination in data systems across the government. Agencies created their own systems based on different standards which meant that information could not be readily shared. These stove-piped systems resulted in higher costs to the government; created inefficiencies; and made it confusing for government workers, vendors, and the public to use the systems.

IAE was initiated to integrate, standardize, and streamline some of the many different acquisition data systems used throughout the government. The program was charged with identifying how information systems could be used to integrate the acquisition functions common to different agencies and to implement governmentwide data systems. Common

---

[1]The Chief Acquisitions Officers Council provides a senior-level forum for monitoring and improving the federal acquisition system.

acquisition functions include, for example, posting contract opportunities, registering contractors who are interested in doing business with the government, assessing contractor past performance, and tracking and reporting contract actions. Bringing disparate data systems together and providing a shared services resource to enter and retrieve acquisition information should help to eliminate unnecessary and repetitive steps in the acquisition process and reduce information technology costs.

When IAE began, OMB directed GSA to execute and manage the initiative. GSA officials said that they worked with other government agencies that would use IAE's systems and established a collaborative governance structure that would allow agency users to set the initiative's priorities and budget. The Acquisition Committee for E-Gov (ACE), a subcommittee of the Chief Acquisition Officer's Council, provides overall governance for IAE. The ACE has several responsibilities, including providing strategic direction for IAE, approving IAE's annual budget and work plan, and ensuring IAE investments align with E-Gov business goals. The ACE is currently co-chaired by representatives from the Departments of Defense and Interior.

IAE Has Evolved over Two Stages

IAE has developed in two stages using different acquisition strategies. Initially, GSA focused on establishing a portfolio of standardized governmentwide systems through an acquisition strategy known as "adopt, adapt, acquire." Using this strategy, GSA adopted or adapted existing agency-specific systems for governmentwide use. If there was no viable system that could be adapted or adopted to meet an identified need, GSA acquired a new system. GSA also established an IAE funding strategy that consisted of contributions from agencies that use IAE systems. In 2008, to further eliminate redundancy, reduce costs, and improve efficiency, GSA began consolidating its portfolio of systems into one integrated system called the System for Award Management (SAM). Unlike the existing systems (sometimes called "legacy" systems) in which a single contractor designed, developed, and operated each of them, IAE relies on multiple vendors to perform these same tasks for SAM. The intent of this approach is to enhance competition and innovation and for the government to own the software associated with the system. SAM will be developed in phases. In each phase, capabilities from selected IAE systems will be added to SAM and those legacy systems will then be shut down.

Initial Strategy Was to Assemble a Portfolio of Standardized Systems

During the first IAE stage, GSA worked to create a portfolio of governmentwide systems through an acquisition strategy known as "adopt, adapt, acquire." GSA and OMB officials surveyed various government stakeholders to develop an inventory of existing data systems and to identify additional data-related needs of the government. Using this information, the ACE directed GSA to adopt or adapt existing agency-specific systems for governmentwide use. For example, the Central Contractor Registration (CCR) database, where contractors register certain business information prior to being considered for contract awards, was a Department of Defense (DOD) system that IAE adopted for governmentwide use in 2003. GSA officials believed DOD's system met the government's requirements, and adopting it was a better alternative than developing a new system. The Federal Procurement Data System – Next Generation (FPDS-NG) is an example of a system that IAE adapted.[2] FPDS, the FPDS-NG predecessor, was initially implemented in 1978 and in 2003 GSA hired a vendor to modernize the system.

When no existing systems could be adopted or adapted for governmentwide use, IAE's strategy was to acquire new systems from software developers. For example, GSA contracted with IBM in 2004 to develop and operate the Online Representations and Certifications Application (ORCA) database, for firms to submit certifications on matters such as firm size and ownership status. Table 1 identifies the portfolio of systems that were included in the first stage of IAE up through 2008 and whether each system was adopted, adapted, or acquired.

---

[2]The Federal Procurement Data System-Next Generation (FPDS-NG) is a database that provides information on government contracting actions over $3,000, procurement trends, and reports on socioeconomic goals.

Table 1: Evolution of the IAE Portfolio

System	Year added to IAE portfolio	Method	Description
Federal Business Opportunities (FedBizOpps)	2003	Adopted/adapted	Single point of entry for solicitations over $25,000, allowing suppliers and government buyers to post, search, monitor, and retrieve federal government market opportunities.
Federal Procurement Data System – Next Generation (FPDS-NG)	2003	Adopted/adapted	Provides public access to data on all federal contract actions over $3,000.
Wage Determinations OnLine (WDOL)	2003	Acquired	Makes Service Contract Act and Davis-Bacon wage determinations accessible by the contracting community.
Past Performance Information Retrieval System (PPIRS)	2003	Adopted/adapted	Provides access to past performance information.
Excluded Parties List System (EPLS)	2005	Adopted/adapted	Identifies parties excluded from receiving federal contracts and certain subcontracts, as well as certain types of federal financial and nonfinancial assistance.
Central Contractor Registration (CCR)	2003	Adopted/adapted	Required point of registration for contractors and grantees wishing to do business with the government.
Federal Agency Registration (FedReg)	2003	Acquired	Single point of information on agency buyers/sellers for intragovernmental transfers.
Electronic Subcontract Reporting System (eSRS)	2005	Acquired	Facilitates prime contractor reporting of accomplishments toward subcontracting goals.
Online Representations and Certifications Application (ORCA)	2004	Acquired	Allows vendors to enter representations and certifications for federal contracts.

Source: GAO analysis of GSA information.

Note: This table lists the systems that were associated with IAE up through 2008. Since then, other systems have been added to the IAE portfolio, including the Federal Awardee Performance and Integrity Information System (FAPIIS) in 2010, the Federal Funding Accountability and Transparency Act Subaward Reporting System (FSRS) in 2010, and the Contractor Performance Assessment Reporting System (CPARS) in 2011. PPIRS was added to the IAE portfolio in 2003, removed in 2005 at the request of the ACE for budgetary reasons, and then added again in 2011.

Shortly after IAE was established, GSA and the ACE created a funding structure in which agencies contribute to the program based on their level of contracting activity. GSA negotiated memorandums of understanding (MOU) with the 24 departments and agencies covered by the Chief Financial Officers Act to collect funding contributions, which pay for the development, operations, and maintenance of IAE's portfolio.[3] When developing its annual budget, GSA estimates what the cost of operating IAE will be and then determines each agency's contribution based on its contracting activity (number and value of contracts) the prior year. For example, DOD is the largest agency in terms of the number and value of contracts awarded and therefore contributes the most, 65 percent of the total.[4] The Federal Funding Accountability and Transparency Act of 2006 (Transparency Act) created new reporting requirements for federal loan and grant recipients that increased the use of certain IAE systems.[5] For example, to comply with the Transparency Act, OMB required grant recipients to register in CCR. In 2008, GSA negotiated separate MOUs with 22 departments and agencies for additional contributions to fund the higher costs associated with providing greater support to grant and loan recipients. Overall, since 2002, about $396 million has been allocated to IAE, as shown in table 2.

Table 2: IAE Memorandum of Understanding (MOU) Contributions and Other Funding, Fiscal Years 2002-2011

Dollars in millions

	2002	2003	2004	2005	2006	2007	2008	2009	2010	2011	Total
Contract MOUs	$7.8	$21.0	$28.6	$34.9	$36.3	$38.7	$39.7	$40.8	$41.3	$42.6	**$331.9**
Grant & loan MOUs	n/a	n/a	n/a	n/a	n/a	n/a	6.2	6.5	5.2	6.5	24.4
Other funding	16.0	22.7	n/a	n/a	n/a	n/a	1.0	n/a	n/a	n/a	39.7
Total	**$23.8**	**$43.8**	**$28.6**	**$34.9**	**$36.3**	**$38.7**	**$47.0**	**$47.3**	**$46.5**	**$49.1**	**$396.0**

Source: GAO analysis of GSA information.

Note: The "Other funding" amounts in 2002 and 2003 were from GSA's General Supply Fund plus a small amount from OMB and the Peace Corps. The 2008 amount was from OMB.

[3] The Chief Financial Officers Act of 1990 (Pub. L. No. 101-576) was the beginning of a series of management reform legislation to improve the general financial management of the federal government. Among other things, it created the position of chief financial officer for certain federal departments and agencies; currently, there are 24 federal chief financial officers.

[4] DOD's contribution is capped at 65 percent of the total contributions. DOD pays 65 percent or its proportional share based on the number and value of its contracts, whichever is less. GSA officials said that DOD has had more than 65 percent of the contracting activity each year so it has always paid 65 percent of the contributions.

[5] Pub. L. No. 109-282.

Another key component that supports the IAE systems is GSA's contract with Dun & Bradstreet for the use of the Data Universal Numbering System (DUNS) and other services to verify and standardize information on contract, grant, and loan recipients. GSA uses the DUNS numbers as unique identifiers for organizing and tracking these entities, including making linkages between parent and subsidiary businesses, within and across the IAE systems. The federal government has used DUNS numbers since 1978, and the Federal Acquisition Regulation (FAR) has required all prospective government contractors to obtain DUNS numbers since 1998.[6] Since 2003, OMB has also required prospective grant recipients to obtain DUNS numbers.[7] IAE's contract with Dun & Bradstreet also supports the use of DUNS numbers for other government-wide information systems, such as USASpending.gov.[8] GSA's current contract with Dun & Bradstreet was awarded in 2010 and is valued at over $135 million for up to 8 years. The Dun & Bradstreet contract is the largest IAE contract.

Since 2008, IAE Has Sought to Consolidate Its Portfolio

In December 2008, the ACE approved a proposal to aggregate the IAE data systems into a new System for Award Management (SAM). GSA officials said that while the existing IAE systems had provided benefits, additional efficiencies could be achieved. For example, the systems contained overlapping data, had separate sign-on procedures, and each system had different hardware, software, and helpdesks. Consolidating the IAE portfolio was intended to reduce costs by eliminating redundancy, streamlining acquisition processes, and consolidating infrastructure.

GSA is relying on an acquisition strategy to develop SAM that is different from what it has used in the past when GSA turned to a single contractor to develop, operate, and support each IAE system. SAM will be split into multiple components with separate contractors responsible for (1) system

---

[6] FAR Subpart 4.11 generally requires prospective contractors to register in CCR and FAR § 52.204-7 requires a DUNS number to register in CCR.

[7] Office of Management and Budget Memorandum M-03-16, "OMB Issues Grants Management Policies" (July 15, 2003).

[8] The Federal Funding Accountability and Transparency Act of 2006 required OMB to ensure the existence and operation of a single searchable website that included information on contracts, grants, loans, and other types of federal spending. USAspending.gov was launched in December 2007 to fulfill these requirements.

design and operations, (2) software development, (3) hosting services, and (4) help desk support (see table 3). The new approach to developing SAM is intended to address lessons learned from past IAE systems. Unlike the legacy systems, the government will own the SAM software as open-source code,[9] the system architecture, and all supporting hardware. IAE officials believe that an open-source approach to software and development will result in lower costs to the government because IAE will be able to avoid sole-source modifications to the system and competitively award future enhancement contracts. GSA officials said that in the past, system enhancements were expensive, in part because the incumbent contractors knew that GSA's only alternative to a sole-source enhancement contract was to develop a new system. Also, GSA officials said the plan to consolidate help desk services into one single contractor is an effective way to control cost and service levels.

---

[9]GSA's definition of open-source code refers to making any custom developed software and associated documentation for SAM publicly available and accessible to other contractors.

Table 3: SAM Contractors and Contracts

Component	Contractor	Contract terms	Description
System Design & Operations	IBM	Fixed-price, service contract awarded in February 2010 for $74 million over 8 years—3 base years and 5 option years	This contractor is responsible for developing the overall system architecture, migrating legacy systems into SAM, and operating and maintaining SAM.
Consolidated Hosting Service	Qwest	Fixed-price service contract awarded in November 2010 under Networx, a GSA multiagency contract, for $3.3 million over 5 years.	This contractor will be responsible for providing the hosting facility for the SAM system and all data, which will be stored on government-owned hardware.
Software Development	Global Computer Enterprises (GCE) (Phase 1) (other contracts to be awarded for later phases)	Fixed-price contract awarded in July 2011 for $1.2 million over 8 months.	Each phase of SAM development will require additional software. The software for each phase will be contracted separately and competitively. As new system requirements are developed, additional contracts will be awarded.
Help Desk (known as Federal Service Desk)	Hewlett- Packard (HP)[a]	Awarded as a fixed- price contract in March 2009 for 5 years—1 base year and 4 option years. The estimated amount of the contract was $2.3 million.	SAM users will be supported by a single help desk, which will assist with tasks such as contractor registration and bid submission.

Source: GAO analysis of GSA information.

[a]Electronic Data Systems (EDS) initially was awarded the contract but was acquired by Hewlett-Packard after the contract award.

With SAM, the system design contractor (IBM) will be responsible for developing the system architecture, defining technical requirements, specifying data migration procedures for each of the legacy systems, and operating and maintaining SAM. Once IBM has specified the technical requirements and data migration procedures for the legacy systems, a second contractor will be responsible for writing the software code that will make up SAM. GCE will write the code for the first phase and GSA will competitively award software contracts for the subsequent phases. IBM will then test and validate the software, implement the system migration, and begin operating and maintaining the new SAM system. A third contractor (Qwest) will provide hosting services, which involves providing a secure facility to physically house SAM and power and Internet connectivity. GSA will provide the hardware (hard drives, servers, and other equipment) and software (operating system, databases, and other software licenses) for the hosting facility. Finally, a fourth contractor (HP) will be responsible for providing a consolidated help desk to support SAM users.

GSA initially planned to migrate IAE systems to SAM in four phases based on groups of legacy IAE systems (see table 4).

Table 4: Initial SAM Development Phases (as of June 2010)

Phases	Systems to be consolidated	Planned completion date
1	CCR, ORCA, EPLS	December 2011
2	FedBizOpps, CFDA, eSRS	March 2012
3	WDOL	July 2012
4	FPDS-NG	February 2014

Source: GSA.

Note: While not part of the IAE portfolio, the Catalog of Federal Domestic Assistance (CFDA) is a system that will become part of a consolidated IAE data system.

GSA and ACE officials viewed a phased approach as having less risk than replacing all the legacy systems at the same time. The timing of each phase was generally established to coincide with expiring legacy system contracts. As each phase is completed, the capabilities of the systems in that phase will be added to SAM and the legacy systems will be shut down. As discussed above, each development phase requires contributions from the four SAM contractors, with GSA managing the various contracts. GSA officials anticipate that additional systems may be added to SAM in the future. For example, the contract with IBM includes an option to migrate the Past Performance Information Retrieval System (PPIRS), which provides access to past performance information on contractors, to SAM. In addition, FedReg has been merged with the Central Contractor Registration (CCR) and will be included in phase 1.

Progress Made in Developing SAM, but Cost Increases and Schedule Delays Could Jeopardize Program Completion

GSA and its contractors have made progress in developing SAM and phase 1 is scheduled to be completed in May 2012. GSA also has worked with contractors to establish a hosting center for the system and a help desk to support users. However, since 2009, the costs of developing SAM have grown significantly. The higher development costs were primarily due to the failure to adequately execute the SAM hosting strategy as initially planned. To a lesser extent, external factors, including recent statutory requirements and policy changes, have contributed to higher operational costs as well by increasing the demand for help desk services. While IAE costs were increasing, the program also experienced a significant funding shortage in fiscal years 2011 and 2012. In response to rising costs and resource constraints, GSA officials have delayed

SAM's development schedule and taken other actions to reduce or defer other costs.

GSA Has Made Progress in Developing SAM

GSA has made progress in consolidating the IAE systems. Specifically, phase 1 of SAM is nearly complete and GSA has created a consolidated hosting environment and established a single help desk called the Federal Service Desk (FSD). GSA and its contractor, IBM, have completed the overarching design of SAM as well as the phase 1 technical requirements. GSA officials also report that the agency has purchased the hosting hardware and software needed for phase 1 and IBM is preparing to make the hosting facility operational in time to launch phase 1. Phase 1 is scheduled to go live in May 2012 and will replace three IAE systems—CCR, ORCA, and EPLS. Officials report that the phase 1 software developer is currently working closely with IBM to coordinate the testing and validation of the phase 1 software. IBM has begun developing the phase 2 requirements and GSA is in the process of competing the phase 2 software development contract. Phase 3 efforts have not yet begun. GSA officials told us FSD currently provides help desk services for most of the IAE data systems. Help desk responsibility for three systems remains with their legacy vendors. GSA officials expect help desk services for these remaining systems to transition to FSD as they become part of SAM.

IAE Has Experienced Cost Growth

Costs of the various SAM components have increased significantly over the past 3 years. GSA did not develop a formal cost baseline when SAM development was started, so we compared the initial contract value for each of the SAM components to the current contract estimates.[10] GSA currently estimates that the various SAM-related contracts will cost $181.1 million. This represents an increase of $85 million, nearly 90 percent, over the initial contract award amounts which totaled about $96 million (see fig. 1).

---

[10]In lieu of a program baseline, IAE program officials referred us to the independent government estimates GSA prepared prior to the solicitation of each contract. After reviewing the initial estimates and discussing them with GSA officials, we believed that comparing the initial contract price award to the current contract cost estimates more accurately reflects the cost growth for each SAM component. Specifically, GSA officials said that they believed the initial estimate for the IBM contract was overstated and the contract was awarded for a much lower price. The initial cost estimate for the contract was about $117 million, but the actual contract award was for $74 million.

Figure 1: Cost Growth for the SAM Components

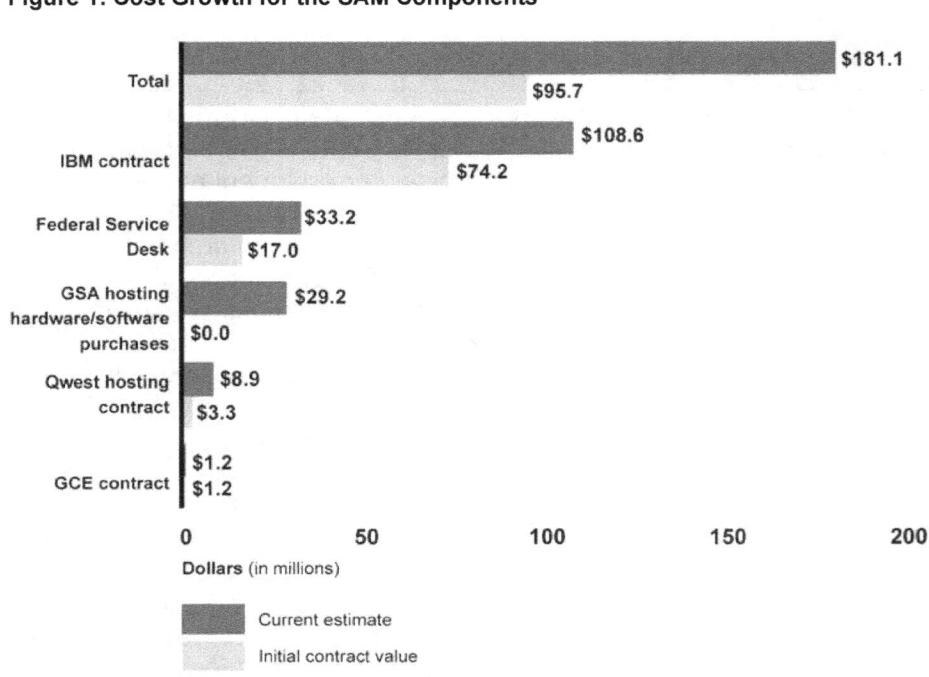

Source: GAO analysis of GSA information.

Most of the cost growth, about $65 million, is due to higher than expected hosting costs. Hosting consists of a secure facility with Internet connectivity; the hardware on which the system will be installed; the operating system and other software necessary to operate the code that will make up SAM; and the operation and maintenance of the hosting environment. GSA estimated in 2008 that hosting costs for the IAE systems were $2.8 million and that annual costs would be much less than that after moving to a single hosting environment. However, we estimate that SAM hosting costs will average $8 million to $9 million per year. The higher costs are largely due to GSA omitting key components from its contracting strategy for acquiring hosting services. GSA's initial strategy was to contract with a single company for all of these hosting services. However, shortly after beginning SAM development, IAE awarded a contract (to Qwest) for a more limited set of hosting services that only included the hosting facility and Internet connectivity.[11] It is not clear why GSA did not include the hosting hardware, software, and operation and maintenance services that were needed. Program officials told us that at the time they believed that the multiagency telecommunications contract used to obtain hosting services from Qwest did not offer the comprehensive services that were needed. Officials also said they thought IBM was responsible for providing these items, but later realized that was not the case. GSA decided to purchase the hosting hardware and software itself under existing GSA schedule contracts at an estimated cost of $29 million. After negotiations with IBM, GSA modified IBM's contract in June 2011, adding $36 million to the $74 million contract price to have IBM install and operate and maintain the hosting hardware and software in Qwest's facility. It took GSA more than a year to finalize its current hosting approach and program officials said they have purchased hosting hardware and software through 13 different contracts instead of just 1 contract as intended under their original hosting strategy.

The help desk function, FSD, also experienced cost growth over its first years of operation as the expected cost has nearly doubled to $33 million. Most of this growth appears to have resulted from factors outside of GSA's control. GSA officials told us the FSD contract price is driven by the amount of support activity provided under the contract. The higher costs reflect a greater than expected demand associated primarily with one data system, CCR. This system serves as a registry for any organization that wants to do business with the federal government. Several events occurred that substantially increased the number of CCR help desk calls. Both the Federal Funding Accountability and Transparency Act of 2006 (Transparency Act) and the American Recovery and Reinvestment Act of 2009 (Recovery Act) included provisions that increased or had the effect of increasing the number of CCR registrants. Specifically, the Transparency Act contained requirements for a single searchable website with data on federal loan, grant, and contract recipients, which prompted the government to require grant recipients to register in CCR.[12] The Recovery Act temporarily

---

[11]Qwest is providing services under a multiagency telecommunications contract available for governmentwide use, known as Networx, which is managed by GSA and offers federal agencies an opportunity to acquire telecommunications services by placing orders against the contract.

[12]In 2003 OMB directed federal agencies to require grantees to get DUNS numbers in order to apply for federal grants. Grantees were not required to register in CCR at that time, but were directed to do so by OMB in August 2010.

increased the number of loan and grant recipients, which also led to greater numbers of CCR registrants. Also, in late 2008, the CCR login process changed in response to actions taken by DOD to improve password security measures. As a result of these changes, there was a drastic rise in help desk activity from CCR customers.

Cost Growth and Resource Constraints Prompted GSA to Delay the SAM Schedule and Defer Costs

While SAM costs were beginning to increase, the program also did not receive funding increases it requested. Up through fiscal year 2010, IAE was primarily funded through agency contributions. When the ACE approved SAM development in 2008, program officials believed that agency contributions would be sufficient to cover the development costs. However, GSA had underestimated its funding needs and soon after the start of SAM development, GSA officials recognized that the amount of agency contributions was insufficient to pay to operate the existing IAE systems and develop SAM over the next several years. GSA officials told us they consulted with OMB and considered various funding options to pay for the development of SAM, including increased agency contributions, a separate appropriation request, or user fees. Ultimately, with OMB's support, GSA decided to seek additional funding through an appropriation and requested $15 million for fiscal year 2011. The program received $7 million of the requested amount.[13] GSA also requested a $38 million appropriation in fiscal year 2012 for SAM, but did not receive any appropriations from Congress for the year. GSA has made a $21 million appropriation request for fiscal year 2013.

GSA officials responded to rising costs and limited resources by modifying and delaying the SAM schedule, and deferring payments or reducing contract requirements where possible. One of the most significant changes was GSA's decision to not transition FPDS-NG to the SAM contract as an interim step prior to FPDS-NG being fully integrated

---

[13]IAE does not have its own appropriation account. IAE appropriation requests have come through GSA's Office of Governmentwide Policy.

into SAM.[14] Under the SAM design contract, FPDS-NG was scheduled to be transitioned in June 2010 from the FPDS-NG legacy contractor to IBM. IBM then would have been responsible for operating and maintaining FPDS-NG "as-is" under the SAM contract and GSA could have ended the FPDS-NG legacy contract. GSA officials said that the transition did not occur because they had neglected to account for the hardware and software required to host FPDS-NG in the new SAM hosting facility and could not afford to buy these components. Instead, GSA awarded a follow-on contract to the FPDS-NG legacy contractor that cost an unanticipated $5.4 million in fiscal year 2011 and is expected to cost another $3.8 million in fiscal year 2012 and a similar amount annually through 2015.[15]

GSA also delayed the schedule for moving the other IAE systems to SAM. In 2010, GSA expected to complete all of the development phases of SAM in early 2014, but under the current schedule the final phase will be completed in 2015, 20 months later than planned (see fig. 2).

---

[14]GSA refers to the process of incorporating capabilities of a system into SAM as "migrating" that system. GSA also envisioned an optional intermediate step which it refers to as "transitioning." Transitioning a system would entail continuing to operate the system "as-is," except that it would be moved to the SAM hosting facility and operated by IBM instead of the legacy contractor. All of the IAE systems will be migrated, but GSA gave IBM discretion as to which systems would be transitioned. When IBM's contract was awarded, the company was required to develop a plan for which systems would be transitioned. FPDS-NG was the only program that IBM initially selected for transition.

[15]GSA also modified the IBM contract to remove responsibility for transitioning FPDS-NG and reduced the contract price by $2 million.

Figure 2: SAM Schedule Delays by Phase

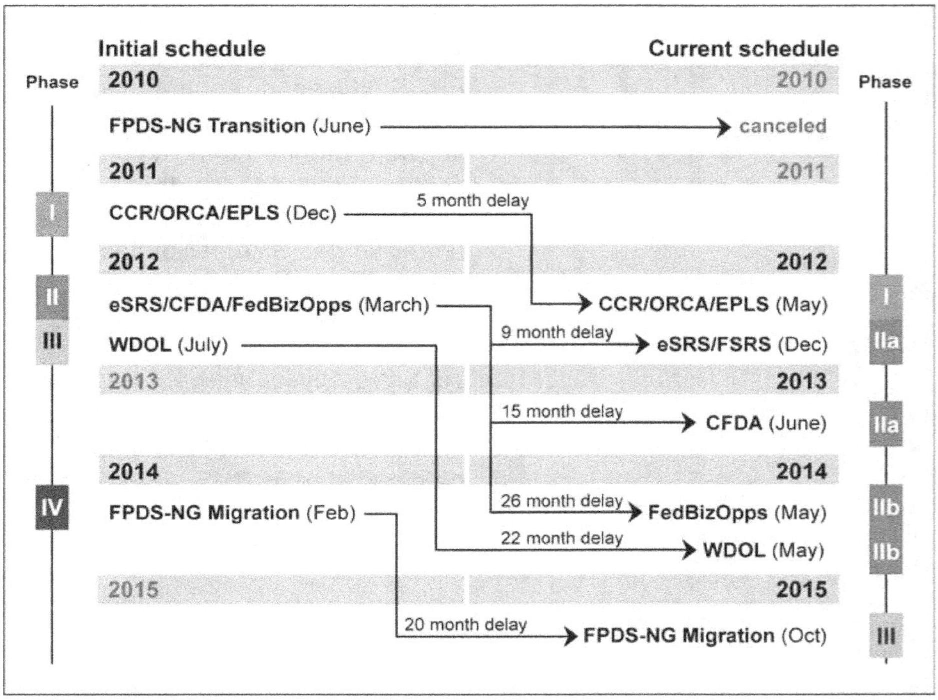

Source: GAO analysis of GSA information.

There was a 5-month delay in implementing phase 1. Delays for phases 2 and 3 are much longer, and GSA officials cited the higher costs for hosting services as the main reason for delaying the phases. Phase 2 has also recently been split into subphases.[16] While the systems included in phase 2a have been delayed for several months, GSA officials said they can complete this phase with available resources because the systems in phase 2a will not require a significant investment in hosting hardware and software. Phase 2b will not be completed until mid-2014, approximately 2 years later than originally planned, in part because GSA cannot afford the estimated $21 million necessary to complete the phase. Furthermore, the migration of FPDS-NG is not scheduled to be completed until 20 months later than planned, in 2015.

---

[16]Phase 2a includes CFDA and eSRS/FSRS. Phase 2b includes FedBizOpps and WDOL.

In addition to delaying SAM's development schedule, GSA officials said they have taken other steps to defer or reduce costs. In 2011, GSA modified the payment schedule for the Dun & Bradstreet DUNS contract to delay payments from fiscal year 2011 to fiscal year 2012. Under the original contract, GSA was scheduled to make an $18 million payment in August 2011. To free up funds in fiscal year 2011, GSA negotiated a modification with Dun & Bradstreet that allowed GSA to pay only $3.8 million in 2011 and deferred the remaining payments to later years. In addition, GSA cut FSD costs by reducing the required level of services stated in the contract. For instance, GSA capped the number of calls the contractor needs to respond to every month, which program officials said has reduced costs and made it easier to estimate future costs. However, the cap on calls may reduce the responsiveness of the help desk to users.[17] GSA officials said they also stopped making investments in the legacy systems and stopped making all but the most minor of changes to the systems. For example, GSA officials said they would fix hyperlinks on the system websites and make other small corrections, but would avoid making larger changes to the legacy systems unless absolutely necessary.

Consequences of Higher SAM Development Costs Threaten IAE Going Forward

Schedule delays and other GSA actions taken in response to cost growth and funding shortages are likely to lead to further cost increases that pose a risk to IAE. Delaying the SAM schedule will require GSA to continue operating the legacy IAE systems, in some cases for years longer than originally expected. At the same time, GSA must contend with higher hosting and help desk costs that will extend over several more years. While GSA has taken some steps to reduce these costs, it has not reevaluated whether its current acquisition strategy, including its approach to acquire hosting services, is still the most cost-effective approach to implement SAM. In addition, although the SAM development phases have been pushed out several years, GSA has not modified its development contract with IBM to reflect these changes. The program continues to pay the same fixed-price amount to the contractor for system development activities as well as operation and maintenance of SAM, even though there was little to operate and maintain for the first 2 years of development.

---

[17]GSA officials said that the first 23,000 calls each month must be answered according to the service agreement in the contract. For any calls above that amount, the contractor may answer them, but is not required to.

Increased IAE Costs Challenge Program

GSA delayed the SAM development schedule in response to cost growth and reduced funding, but those delays will result in additional cost increases as GSA has to extend the life of the legacy systems. For example, the decision to not transition FPDS-NG to the IBM contract as originally planned could increase GSA's costs by approximately $16 million as GSA will have to continue operating FPDS-NG for 5 years longer than expected.[18] Similarly, the 2-year delay in migrating FedBizOpps into SAM means that GSA will have to spend $2.8 million on FedBizOpps in fiscal year 2012. Assuming costs remain the same, continuing to operate FedBizOpps for 2 additional years will increase costs by approximately $5.6 million. Schedule delays may also increase FSD costs. GSA officials said that the majority of the help desk calls are associated with CCR whose migration has been delayed 5 months. In addition to paying the CCR legacy vendor to continue operating CCR for 5 additional months, GSA will also have to pay the FSD vendor to continue supporting CCR.

GSA is also grappling with higher SAM development costs, but has not assessed whether its current acquisition approach is still cost-effective. For example, GSA abandoned its initial hosting strategy without evaluating the cost or schedule implications of doing so. The initial strategy to use a single contractor to provide consolidated hosting services was intended to achieve cost savings, but the revised approach, which relies on multiple contractors, has proven to be much more costly than expected and led to schedule delays. Hosting costs are now a primary impediment to moving forward because GSA cannot afford to purchase the hardware and software necessary to complete phases 2 and 3. In addition, according to program officials, GSA efforts to procure hosting hardware and software have resulted in 13 different contracts, the management of which has required additional program support resources.

GSA also continues to pay the SAM development contractor, IBM, essentially the same amount called for in the original contract even

---

[18]Operating FPDS-NG will cost approximately $20.8 million over 5 years—$5.4 million in 2011 and approximately $3.8 million annually for fiscal years 2012 through 2015. This will be partially offset by savings of approximately $5 million that resulted from GSA modifying IBM's contract to remove responsibility for FPDS-NG. However, the net reduction in the IBM contract was only $2 million because GSA added in $2.9 million in additional services related to EPLS and ORCA.

though schedule delays have pushed work out into the future. IBM's contract includes responsibility for designing as well as operating and maintaining SAM. According to the fixed-price contract, SAM will be developed in phases, yet the payment schedule specified that IBM was to be paid a set amount each month (approximately 3 percent of the total contract price) for all activities under the 36-month base contract. This payment schedule may have been appropriate under GSA's initial plan, but the development schedule changed shortly after the contract was awarded and much of the work to migrate systems into SAM will occur much later than planned. While the SAM transition and migration schedules have changed considerably, GSA has not adjusted IBM's payment schedule to reflect the current development schedule.[19] For example, IBM was not responsible for operating any IAE systems until the Excluded Parties List System (EPLS) was transitioned to the SAM contract in July 2011—17 months into the contract. By that time, GSA had already paid IBM $6.3 million of the $20.3 million contract price for SAM operation and maintenance. GSA and IBM officials noted that payments to date have been for planning and preparing to migrate the legacy systems to SAM. However, under the original schedule, IBM would have performed these services as well as operated FPDS-NG for the same cost. Similarly, GSA has paid more than half of the contract price for phase 2 migration activities even though phase 2 is not scheduled to be completed until May 2014.[20]

We raised issues about the increasing cost with SAM, and the viability of the hosting approach and the development contract structure with GSA officials and they recently told us that GSA has initiated an internal review, called a TechStat, of IAE.[21] A TechStat is intended to be an evidence-based review of underperforming information technology investment during which agency leadership reviews a program, examines

---

[19]Program officials said that during negotiations with IBM to remove the FPDS-NG transition, GSA did receive consideration for certain work that was scheduled but not performed during the first 2 years of the contract.

[20]GSA restructured its phases so the systems that were initially in phases 2 and 3 were combined into phase 2. Subsequently, phase 2 was divided into phases 2a and 2b. For phase 2a, eSRS and FSRS are scheduled to be migrated to SAM in December 2012 and CFDA is scheduled for migration in June 2013. Phase 2b (FedBizOpps and WDOL) is scheduled for completion in May 2014.

[21]In December 2010, OMB called on agency CIOs to implement TechStats in order to turn around or terminate one-third of poorly performing projects in their portfolio.

performance, and develops corrective actions as necessary. Program officials said their current focus is on completing phase 1 of SAM, but they may revisit their hosting strategy once the phase is completed. GSA officials also told us that they will begin negotiating with IBM to change the contract to reflect current schedule changes and available funding.

Conclusions

GSA's effort to consolidate the IAE legacy systems into SAM has the potential to reduce agency costs, eliminate redundancy, and streamline government acquisition processes. Two years into development, however, SAM is in trouble due to higher costs that planned funding levels do not cover. Most of the cost growth seen to date is largely the result of mistakes the program made. Rather than using a consolidated hosting strategy as initially proposed, the program adopted a piecemeal approach involving multiple sources that will cost about $65 million more than expected. The need for additional resources to cover the increase in hosting costs, however, coincided with significant funding shortfalls in the past 2 years and now the program cannot afford to develop SAM as planned.

Despite dramatically different circumstances marked by higher costs and constrained resources, GSA has not reassessed its business case for SAM. Specifically, GSA has not assessed whether developing SAM is still a better option than maintaining the status quo or whether the current development strategy, involving multiple vendors, is more cost-effective than using a single vendor. Ensuring there is a sound business case for moving forward will be critical before establishing an acquisition strategy to address the program's problems. Also, while GSA has taken steps to reduce costs, by delaying development and deferring some costs to the future, there may be more that can be done to stretch available resources. For example, in light of higher hosting costs than expected, GSA has not reevaluated whether its hosting strategy is the most cost-effective approach. In addition, GSA has not modified the primary SAM development contract to align payments with program schedule delays. Although GSA officials recently indicated they will begin negotiating changes to the development contract, it continues to pay the contractor for operation and maintenance activities even though many of the IAE systems will not be migrated into SAM for several years. Tying contract payments to the migration of the data systems and schedule milestones would ensure that the government is not paying for work that has not yet been accomplished.

Recommendations for Executive Action

To ensure that GSA has a sound approach for providing IAE services in the future, we recommend that the Administrator of GSA take the following two actions:

- Reassess the SAM business case to compare the costs and benefits of various alternatives such as:
  - terminating SAM development and continuing to operate the legacy systems,
  - maintaining the current acquisition approach to developing SAM,
  - pursuing a different acquisition strategy for SAM, such as using a single contractor to develop and operate the system.

- If the results of this assessment support continuing the current acquisition approach, then:
  - reevaluate the hosting strategy to ensure that it is the most cost-effective approach that can be supported with available resources, and
  - take steps to ensure that the SAM development contract payments are more closely aligned with the program schedule and delivery of capabilities.

Agency Comments and Our Evaluation

We provided a draft of this report to GSA and OMB. In its written comments, GSA concurred with our recommendations and indicated that it will take appropriate action. GSA added that it has established an integrated project team that will reassess and develop a broad plan covering both SAM and the IAE program as a whole. GSA's written comments appear in appendix III. GSA also provided technical comments that we incorporated, as appropriate. OMB informed us that it did not have comments on the draft.

We are sending copies of this report to interested congressional committees, the Administrator of General Services and the Director of the Office of Management and Budget. In addition, this report will be available at no charge on the GAO website at http://www.gao.gov.

If you or your staff have questions about this report, please call me at (202) 512-4841. Contact points for our Offices of Congressional Relations and Public Affairs may be found on the last page of this report. GAO staff who made major contributions to this report are listed in appendix IV.

William T. Woods
Director
Acquisition and Sourcing Management

Appendix I: Scope and Methodology

To determine how the General Services Administration (GSA) developed the Integrated Acquisition Environment (IAE) initiative, we interviewed IAE officials and analyzed relevant documents. Specifically, we interviewed former and current IAE officials and the two Acquisition Committee for E-Gov (ACE) co-chairs from the Departments of Defense and Interior. These individuals described the acquisition strategy and governance structure that IAE developed in its early years. We verified these accounts with historical documents, such as internal newsletters and minutes from the ACE meetings that documented IAE's development. To learn about the acquisition strategy IAE used to develop the System for Award Management (SAM), we interviewed IAE officials, reviewed IAE presentations, and analyzed SAM contract documents. We interviewed officials from IAE and the Office of Management and Budget (OMB) to learn about the program's funding arrangement, obtained historical funding documents, and reviewed four of the interagency memorandums of understanding (MOU) used to fund IAE.

To determine the progress IAE has made in implementing SAM, we interviewed IAE officials and two of the contractors that are implementing SAM—IBM and GCE. We also reviewed IAE presentations, agency memorandums and communications, and analyzed SAM-related contracts. Due to lack of a formal cost baseline when SAM development started, we focused on the growth of the individual contracts of SAM, such as the IBM contract and the help desk contract. To determine SAM's schedule growth, we used the original schedule created by IBM shortly after the contract was awarded and compared that to the latest schedule IAE officials provided us.

To understand and analyze the challenges IAE is facing in their consolidation, we interviewed officials from GSA, IAE, and OMB and analyzed SAM-related contracts. We also discussed IAE's acquisition strategy with information technology contractors such as IBM and GCE. In order to understand IAE's budget issues, we analyzed budget documents identifying projected funding and expenditures. We also analyzed the structure of IBM's contract and verified our findings with IAE officials.

We conducted this performance audit from September 2011 to March 2012 in accordance with generally accepted government auditing standards. Those standards require that we plan and perform the audit to obtain sufficient, appropriate evidence to provide a reasonable basis for our findings and conclusions based on our audit objectives. We believe that the evidence obtained provides a reasonable basis for our findings and conclusions based on our audit objectives.

Appendix II: Integrated Acquisition Environment (IAE) Data Systems

Data system	Central Contractor Registration (CCR)
Description	CCR originally was a Department of Defense (DOD) data system that was brought into the Integrated Acquisition Environment (IAE) portfolio in 2003 and adapted for use across the federal government. CCR is the primary registrant database for the U.S. government. The government uses CCR to collect, validate, store, and disseminate data in support of agency acquisition and award missions. According to the Federal Acquisition Regulation, prospective contractors must register in CCR prior to the award of a contract. Also, to register in CCR, a firm must have a Dun & Bradstreet Data Universal Number System (DUNS) number.
Vendor information	The General Services Administration (GSA) has a contract with Northrop Grumman Information Technology to operate and maintain CCR. This contract ends September 2012.
Data system	Electronic Subcontracting Reporting System (eSRS)
Description	The Electronic Subcontract Reporting System (eSRS) was created in 2005 and intended to streamline the small business subcontracting program reporting process and provide the data to agencies in a manner that will enable them to more effectively manage the program. The Small Business Administration partnered with the IAE and other agency partners to develop the eSRS system. The eSRS is an Internet-based reporting tool that eliminates the need for contractors to submit and process Individual Subcontracting Reports (SF 294) and Summary Subcontracting Reports (SF 295) in hard copy. In 2007, the eSRS implemented an interface with FPDS-NG, which permits contractors to enter a contract number into eSRS and have the contract data retrieved from FPDS-NG for use in the subcontracting reports.
Vendor information	IAE has a contract with Symplicity, the original developer of eSRS, to provide operation and maintenance of eSRS. This contract will expire in September 2012, and IAE has plans to enter an interim contract with the same vendor until the system is migrated to SAM.
Data system	Excluded Parties List System (EPLS)
Description	The purpose of EPLS is to provide a single comprehensive list of individuals and firms excluded from receiving federal contracts or federally approved subcontracts and from certain types of federal financial and nonfinancial assistance and benefits. Contracting officers

GAO-12-429 Federal Contracting

	use EPLS to determine whether to enter into a transaction with a specific contractor. EPLS is also available to the general public.
Vendor information	In 2011, IBM assumed responsibility to maintain and operate EPLS under the System for Award Management (SAM) contract.
Data system	Federal Business Opportunities (FedBizOpps)
Description	FedBizOpps is the single point of entry for federal buyers to publish and for vendors to find federal business opportunities over $25,000 across departments and agencies. Vendors can conduct ad hoc searches or set up automatic queries to notify them when opportunities meeting their criteria are posted.
Vendor information	IAE has a contract with Symplicity to operate and maintain FedBizOpps. IAE plans to exercise the two option years on the current contract, signed in 2011, and to extend it again until FedBizOpps is migrated to SAM.
Data system	Federal Agency Registration (FedReg)
Description	In response to GAO's classification of intragovernmental transactions as a governmentwide material weakness, OMB and the IAE collaborated with DOD to create FedReg in 2003. FedReg collects standard data on federal agency buyers and sellers who perform intragovernmental transactions. FedReg sends data on buyers and sellers to the Intragovernmental Transaction Exchange and Intragovernmental Transaction System to assist in tracking all intragovernmental transactions. FedReg also serves as a sort of government "Yellow Pages," providing information on federal sellers of goods and services. All federal entities engaged in intragovernmental buying or selling must be registered. FedReg is now embedded within CCR.
Vendor information	GSA has a contract with Northrop Grumman Information Technology to operate and maintain FedReg (and CCR). This contract ends September 2012.
Data system	Federal Procurement Data System – Next Generation (FPDS-NG)
Description	The Federal Procurement Data System-Next Generation is a database that provides information on government contracting actions over $3,000, procurement trends, and achievement of socioeconomic goals, such as small business participation. In fiscal year 2011, there were nearly

	17,000,000 transactions recorded in FPDS-NG. FPDS-NG has been the primary governmentwide contracting database since 1978, and it serves as the backbone for other government contracting data systems. Since 1982, GSA has administered the database on behalf of the Office of Federal Procurement Policy.
Vendor information	GSA awarded the FPDS-NG contract to Global Computer Enterprises, Inc., in 2011, and can exercise option years through 2015.
Data system	Wage Determinations OnLine.Gov (WDOL)
Description	WDOL provides a single location for federal contracting officers to obtain Service Contract Act and Davis-Bacon Act wage determinations. These acts require contractors and subcontractors to pay no less than the locally prevailing wages for services contracts and public works projects. In addition to wage determinations, the site also provides information on labor standards, federal and agency acquisition regulations, agency contracting processes, and other related information.
Vendor information	WDOL is physically maintained by the National Technical Information Service, an agency of the Department of Commerce.
Data system	Online Representations and Certifications Application (ORCA)
Description	This application enables prospective government contractors to electronically submit required certifications and representations for responses to government solicitations for all federal contracts, instead of using hard copies for individual awards. The representations and certifications can be considered current for up to one year. These representations and certifications include certifications of socioeconomic status, affirmative action compliance, and compliance with veterans' employment reporting requirements.
Vendor information	IBM has been the vendor for ORCA since its inception in 2004. In 2011, IBM assumed responsibility to maintain and operate ORCA under the SAM contract.

Appendix III: Comments from the General Services Administration

GSA Administrator

March 8, 2012

The Honorable Gene L. Dodaro
Comptroller General of the United States
U.S. Government Accountability Office
Washington, DC 20548

Dear Mr. Dodaro:

The U.S. General Services Administration (GSA) appreciates the opportunity to review
and comment on the draft report, "Federal Contracting: Effort to Consolidate
Governmentwide Acquisition Data Systems Should Be Reassessed", (GAO-12-429).
The U.S. Government Accountability Office (GAO) recommends that GSA reassess the
Integrated Acquisition Environment (IAE) business case to determine whether the
current acquisition strategy is the most cost effective alternative and if so, reevaluate
the current hosting strategy and align contract payments with the program schedule.

We agree with the recommendations and will take appropriate action. GSA has
established an Integrated Project Team that will reassess and develop a broad plan
covering both System For Award Management and the IAE program as a whole.
Additional specific actions will be provided upon receipt of the final report. Staff inquiries
may be directed to Ms. Kathleen Turco, Associate Administrator for the Office of
Government-wide Policy. She can be reached at (202) 501-8880.

Sincerely,

Martha Johnson

Martha Johnson
Administrator

cc: William T. Woods

U.S. General Services Administration
1275 First Street, NE
Washington, DC 20417
www.gsa.gov

Appendix IV: GAO Contact and Staff Acknowledgments

GAO Contact	William T. Woods, (202) 512-4841 or WoodsW@gao.gov
Staff Acknowledgments	In addition to the contact name above, John Oppenheim (Assistant Director); Marie Ahearn; E. Brandon Booth; Jillian Fasching; Madhav Panwar; Jeffrey Sanders; Benjamin Shattuck; Roxanna Sun; Robert Swierczek; and Rebecca Wilson made key contributions to this report.

GAO's Mission	The Government Accountability Office, the audit, evaluation, and investigative arm of Congress, exists to support Congress in meeting its constitutional responsibilities and to help improve the performance and accountability of the federal government for the American people. GAO examines the use of public funds; evaluates federal programs and policies; and provides analyses, recommendations, and other assistance to help Congress make informed oversight, policy, and funding decisions. GAO's commitment to good government is reflected in its core values of accountability, integrity, and reliability.
Obtaining Copies of GAO Reports and Testimony	The fastest and easiest way to obtain copies of GAO documents at no cost is through GAO's website (www.gao.gov). Each weekday afternoon, GAO posts on its website newly released reports, testimony, and correspondence. To have GAO e-mail you a list of newly posted products, go to www.gao.gov and select "E-mail Updates."
Order by Phone	The price of each GAO publication reflects GAO's actual cost of production and distribution and depends on the number of pages in the publication and whether the publication is printed in color or black and white. Pricing and ordering information is posted on GAO's website, http://www.gao.gov/ordering.htm. Place orders by calling (202) 512-6000, toll free (866) 801-7077, or TDD (202) 512-2537. Orders may be paid for using American Express, Discover Card, MasterCard, Visa, check, or money order. Call for additional information.
Connect with GAO	Connect with GAO on Facebook, Flickr, Twitter, and YouTube. Subscribe to our RSS Feeds or E-mail Updates. Listen to our Podcasts. Visit GAO on the web at www.gao.gov.
To Report Fraud, Waste, and Abuse in Federal Programs	Contact: Website: www.gao.gov/fraudnet/fraudnet.htm E-mail: fraudnet@gao.gov Automated answering system: (800) 424-5454 or (202) 512-7470
Congressional Relations	Katherine Siggerud, Managing Director, siggerudk@gao.gov, (202) 512-4400, U.S. Government Accountability Office, 441 G Street NW, Room 7125, Washington, DC 20548
Public Affairs	Chuck Young, Managing Director, youngc1@gao.gov, (202) 512-4800 U.S. Government Accountability Office, 441 G Street NW, Room 7149 Washington, DC 20548

www.ingramcontent.com/pod-product-compliance
Lightning Source LLC
Chambersburg PA
CBHW080935290526
45795CB00007BA/2762